HOUSTON ARCHITECTURAL BALLADE

Valentin L. Gertsman

Mills & Morris Publishing
Houston, Texas
2000

To my dearest wife, Joyce, my friend, advisor, first critic, and genius violin teacher, I dedicate this book.

Published with assistance from the Houston Architecture Foundation

Major Underwriter:
Reliant Energy

Underwriters:
Greater Houston Convention and Visitors Bureau
Linbeck Construction Corporation
BMC Software
The Chase Private Bank
Continental Airlines
Crescent Real Estate Equities, Ltd.
Houston Cellular
Kino Studio, Inc.
Texaco
Stephen E. Guilliams, M.D.
Spring Branch Medical Center
Brown & Root a Halliburton Company
Gerald H. Dubin
Houston Chapter Associated General Contractors
Morris Architects
Neider Financial Consultants, Inc.
Ann Wright & Dan Curtis

Mills & Morris Publishing
Houston, Texas

Editor, Gerald Moorhead
Book Coordination, Rita Mills
Book and Cover Design,
    Kelman Design, Houston
Copyeditor, Judy King

Gertsman, Valentin L. Houston architectural
    ballade / by Valentin L. Gertsman.
1st ed.p. cm. Includes index.
LCCN: 99-66675
ISBN: 0-9645493-1-X
1. Architecture--Texas--Houston--Pictorial
works. 2. Houston (Tex.)--Pictorial works.
I. Title.

NA735.H68G47 2000
720i.9764í1411
QB199-1361

The paper used in this publication meets the
requirements of the American National
Standard for Permanence of Paper for Printed
Library Materials Z39.48-1984.

First edition - 5,000 copies

Printed in Hong Kong by Print Network Co.,
Ltd. with Wm Thornton Organization
Richardson, Texas

TO HOUSTON

From Liege, changing airplanes in Geneva and New York, I reached my final destination, Houston. It was early afternoon December 19, 1974, when Barbara Meistrich from the Jewish Family Service drove me from George Bush Intercontinental Airport to a dormitory on the campus of the University of Houston. Here I was, a Russian immigrant, almost without luggage, of course without money, speaking French instead of English, with an uncertain future. Suddenly against a bright blue sky there appeared the breathtaking skyline of downtown! "This is a city of the 21st century," I thought. At that moment, I could not imagine that after six years of pain, loneliness, and terrible nostalgia, I would begin one of the most important projects of my life, photographing this beautiful city, my second home after Moscow.

MY SHORT STORY

Back home in Moscow in the early '30s, inside my little toy box between wooden cubes, metal construction tidbits, and other boyish belongings was a head of Lenin. It was made of greenish clay, hard as rock, and about the size of a goose egg. My mother told me it was my creation, so my relationship with art goes back beyond my own recollection. As a child and later throughout my medical career, drawing portraits and painting watercolors and pastels have been an intermittent part of my life.

I left Moscow for Houston in 1974. Three months after my arrival, I began to work as a surgical assistant at Spring Branch Medical Center. American medical aesthetics amazed me, so I started collecting disposable surgical materials and constructing sculptures. One day in 1978 while cleaning the drawer of my desk, I came across three small branches of wood that my eight-year-old daughter, Julia, and I had found in a forest near Moscow shortly before my departure. The longer I stared at them, the more meaningful they became. I decided to mount those branches on pedestals and apply an oil for protection. That marked the beginning of my "career" as a "driftwood sculptor." Two years later I sold my first sculpture. Before giving it to the purchaser, Bobby Taylor, an international businessman, I decided to take a picture of it for my records. My artist friend Efim Frumin lent me his old Mamiya, and looking at my sculpture through the lens, I realized that photography is an art in itself. With the advice of Dr. Louis Chen, a colleague and expert in cameras, I purchased a Minolta and began photographing my sculptures and scenes of nature.

One morning in 1981, my close friend and talented artist Michael Jorden invited me to go downtown to take pictures. I agreed because Houston's architecture had always fascinated me. This started "architectural theme" in my photography.

Early in December of the same year my colleagues and I were resting between surgeries in the doctors' lounge. Suddenly Dr. Marcel Molina said to me, "Soyuz,* in the lobby of the highrise at 1400 Hermann is a gallery to which I have access. In one week you will have an exhibit there." I was shocked! I had never even dreamed about exhibiting my work, and I responded, "No, it is impossible." But he insisted, and on December 17 my first exhibit was opened.

In May 1984 I opened the newspaper and read that Joan Miró, creator of a downtown sculpture which I had photographed many times, had died. "Real art is immortal," I thought. "Perhaps somebody would like to publish these photos in his memory." I shared this idea with my English teacher, Betty Lou Brecht, and she started making calls. As a result, the fine arts editor of the *Houston Chronicle*, Ann Holmes, published a series of my photographs of downtown Houston (including the Miró sculpture) in the *Texas Magazine* of the *Houston Chronicle* on May 20, 1984. Her cover story, "Houston art goes outdoors: An eye for the abstract," was the first publication about me as a photographer. Since that time, I have called my dear friend Betty "my lucky penny."

*

This book contains photographs based on contemporary architecture and monumental sculptures in the public spaces of Houston. The composite photographs in Chapter Three are abstract and symbolize some of the most important aspects of the city's life as capital of the international oil industry, center of medicine, space exploration, and culture.

Houston, dynamic and constantly growing, is now facing the new millennium as one of the leading modern American cities. For me, architecturally, Houston had reached the 21st century years ago.

Welcome to my Houston!

---

* In 1975 USA & USSR launched the Apollo-Soyuz test project, the first international manned space mission.

A PHOTOGRAPHER OF THE BODY

In Hans Christian Andersen's story, "The Tinder Box," there are three dogs: the first with eyes as large as teacups, the second with eyes as large as millstones, and the third with eyes as large as the round tower. Each one guards a treasure chest. When I was very young, I read this story in a book with a green cover and colored illustrations on shiny paper. One of these illustrations showed the dog with eyes as large as teacups. (The other two would be hard to visualize.) The picture both fascinated and terrified me. The hero of the story is a poor soldier, and in the end the three dogs save his life and find him the princess he wants to marry. They are ferocious guard dogs such as notices on the fences around secret government properties warn about, and they are also dogs of paradise. My fear as well as my fascination before the picture in the green book attracted me in a way which was as mysterious as the dog himself. It was as if this staring animal was my own body, dog of my own body's panic and longing. Guard dog and paradise dog with eyes as large as teacups.

Fifty years later Valentin Gertsman, the photographer, found the same dog on a sidewalk in Houston, Texas (page 8). Or rather he found half of it, made of stains, dribbles, and sunlight on the paving stones, and then by sandwiching slides together and printing it, he had its complete portrait with its eyes as large as teacups, its nose, muzzle, teeth, and its shaggy fur with a suggestion of a dark smell to it.

I speak of it because there is something mysterious about all of Gertsman's work: something which escapes any purely aesthetic explanation, indeed something which resembles a fairy story.

*

When he was 17, in 1943, Gertsman volunteered for the Red Army. Many institutions and places in Russia are changing their names, but the Great Patriotic War against the fascist invaders will remain, I think, the Great Patriotic War. He was sent to the northwest front, south of Leningrad during the terrible and unforgettable siege of that city.

After the war he decided to train to become a doctor. There were, he says, three reasons for this decision. First, in the face of what he had seen on the front, he felt a need to be beside those who suffered. Second, of any profession open to him, medicine was the furthest removed from politics. And third, if he was arrested and sent to the Gulag, as his father was, he would still have the small advantage of being able to practice there as a doctor.

Later he chose to become a surgeon. A surgeon since he had nimble hands and since by nature he was impatient, eager to see swift alleviation.

The years passed. In the 1970s, when Gertsman applied for permission to emigrate to Israel, he asked himself how he would be able to earn his living in the West, supposing his medical qualifications were not recognized there. I could, he reassured himself, be an artist!

He had already begun taking photographs as a way of keeping a record of his "found sculptures." These consisted of small roots or fragments of wood or flotsam which he found on the ground, picked up, mused over, and would sometimes mount on a plinth. These natural sculptures were often erotic and were always reminiscent of parts, members, or organs of the body.

When eventually Gertsman did emigrate, he went straight to the United States and there, in fact, found work as a surgeon in Houston. Taking photographs, however, became one of his greatest passions.

*

For me, the fairy story of his photography still concerns the body.

This may seem strange since his pictures rarely include people and are mostly of metals, stone, water, cement, glass, the occasional branch of a tree, the blue of the sky, buildings, streets. At the same time, it is hard to imagine photos which are less documentary than his. Gertsman is certainly not the Atget of Houston.

His photos of the city which he has adopted remain profoundly Russian. If I wondered about his formal or stylistic companions, I would immediately think of Lissitzsky or Tatlin. The mood of his work, however, is very different. Russian Constructivism in the 1920s was bursting with combative energy. Gertsman's pictures are about a longed-for peace. For all their obvious and textural materiality, they are dreamlike. The puzzle is how to locate their dream.

A clue is given by the photograph entitled "Self-Portrait" (page 6). Like many others, it shows a corner of a park or terrazzo in the Texas oil capital. No more than the photographer's feet and legs are visible. But, surprisingly, he is dressed in his "greens," as if he were in an operating theater!

Imagine all these images as X-rays. But in color. Their spatial perspective is flattened as in an X-ray, and although one never forgets that the shapes represent real physical things, one has the impression of entering, thanks to the angle of vision, into a space that is normally invisible. The city skyline or the surface of a highway is seen as if it were something internal, mysteriously internal to the body of the visible.

In this revealed internal space, all the physical surfaces shown have an organic energy, yet this energy is framed, held by a geometry imposed by the photographer's eye and timing, a geometry which is a kind of ideal intervention, bestowing peace upon that which, because it is organic, cannot be peaceful or cannot remain peaceful.

We watch, and as we watch, the body of the visible becomes our own body. And then the sensation of peace enters us – as if brought there by the dog of paradise.

John Berger

TRIBUTE TO OLD IMAGE

ONE AFTERNOON

One afternoon in the fall of 1988 the curator of architecture of the New York Public Library, while reviewing my Houston portfolio, suddenly hurried away and returned with a book about Dallas, composed mainly of cowboy images. He said that previously his impression of Houston had been the same – "Cowboy City"– but after seeing my work, he changed his opinion. I have never forgotten his remark. That is why I have decided on "TRIBUTE TO OLD IMAGE" as the opening chapter of my book.

"PREPARATION FOR PARADE"
spring of 1983

This photograph was made in downtown Houston in the spring of 1983, the season for the
Houston Livestock Show and Rodeo. The Gus S. Wortham Theater Center now stands on this spot.

GERTSMAN'S ARCHITECTURE

Valentin Gertsman's photography, both the straight shots and the abstract composites, is highly influenced by the architecture of his adopted city. Houston is a new city, largely built since World War II, where buildings are quickly replaced when their economic life has faded. Little remains of the pre-war city and very little of the 19th-century town on the banks of sluggish Buffalo Bayou. By the time Gertsman began taking pictures in the early 1980s, Houston was a boomtown of modern skyscrapers.

The plan of Houston was laid out in the summer of 1836 by the Allen brothers, New York land speculators who arrived at the head of navigation shortly after Sam Houston defeated Santa Anna at nearby San Jacinto. Buying 600 acres of level coastal farmland on the south banks of Buffalo Bayou, John K. and Augustus C. Allen platted a grid of 62 blocks, each 250 feet square. Throughout the 19th and early 20th centuries, Houston looked like any other American city of the period with low-rise, highly ornamented architecture, canopy-covered sidewalks, and eventually trolley cars and power poles.

The architectural effect of the relatively small city grid did not become apparent until the building boom of the 1970s and 1980s when the earlier buildings were replaced with skyscrapers. Given the optimal 25,000-square-foot floor plate of the speculative high-rise office building, only one tower could fit on a city block, surrounded by wide sidewalks and occasionally a small "plaza" with a piece of "civic art." By the end of the century, the grid of downtown has become a virtual three-dimensional extrusion of itself, rows of slender towers rising in monumental isolation directly from the street.

High-rise architecture since the '70s has been an increasingly complex game of geometry, with each new tower vying for identity on the skyline. Architect Philip Johnson's Pennzoil Place of 1976 (page 20) set the style for a minimalist expression of corporate power. Postmodernism of the '80s, with its faux-historical recollections, had little effect on downtown Houston, already deep in recession, leaving a landscape of modernist steel and reflective glass.

The minimalist geometry and pattern of Houston's towers lend themselves to Gertsman's compositional methods. He takes ample advantage of the qualities of the architecture itself: reflection, transparency, repetitive pattern, color, form. The juxtaposition of colorful sculpture against the cool reflections of curtain walls frequently catches Gertsman's lens. Images reversed, overlapped, or mirrored create new geometries of transparency. The strong Gulf Coast light and deep blue sky become as solid or as ephemeral as any of the architectonic elements transformed within Gertsman's frame.

Whether straight shots or the "compositions" of sandwiched slides, Gertsman's photographs are coolly abstract. His non-figural images carry no referential or metaphoric subtext other than whatever their strong visual presence incites in the viewer. His statement is to see beyond what you see to a pure world of form, color, and pattern.

Gerald Moorhead, FAIA

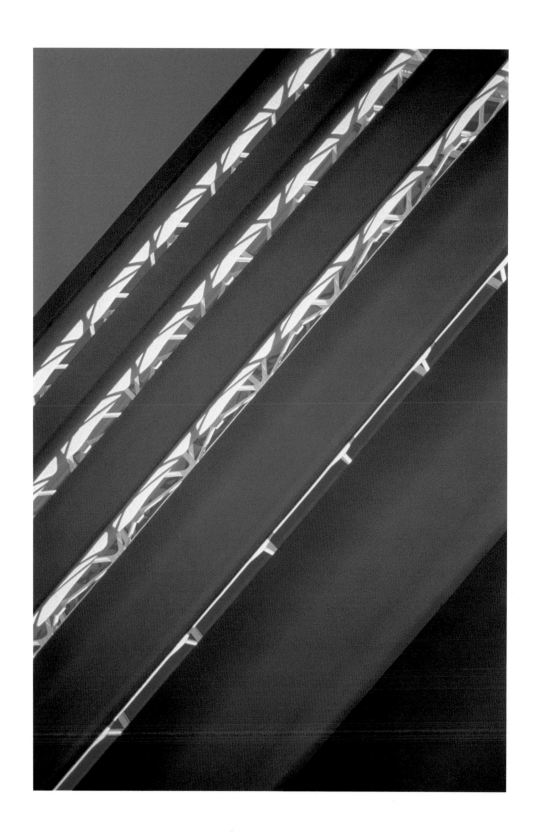

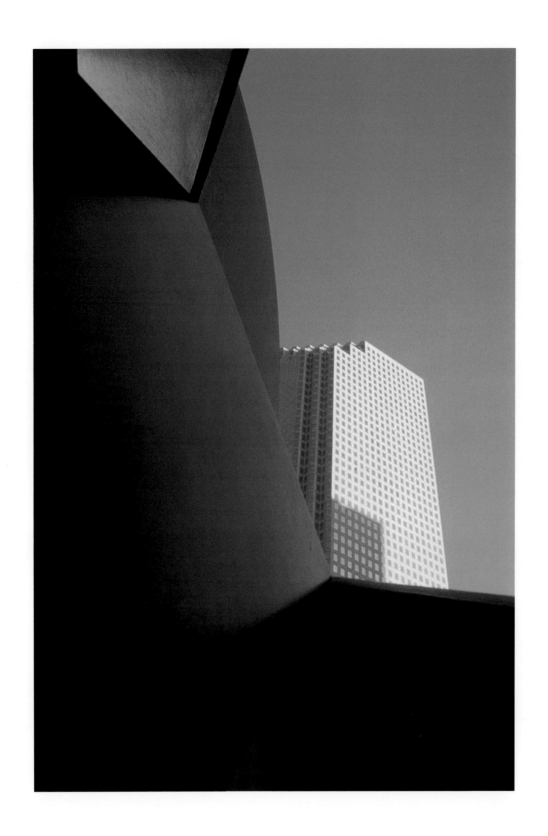

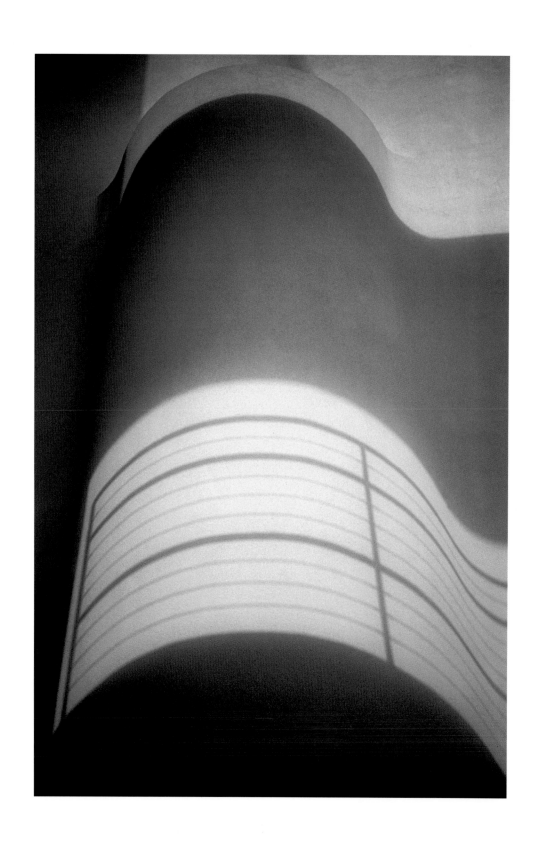

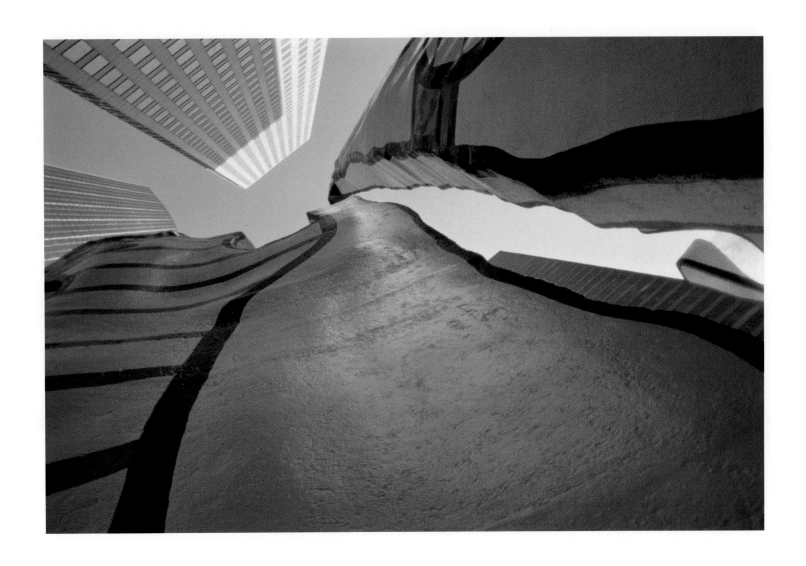

An Architectural Ballad

Cracks in the concrete
Flower life unexpected
Contrasting dead stone
Buildings crouch close
Mirror glass edifices reflect one another
Multiplying their strengths and weaknesses
Skyscrapers collide
Corners jab like sharp elbows
The neutral sky watches
Magical montage
Jazz-like ensemble
Layers of colored light
Knots of steel
Shiny, symmetrical
Visions of a new "Oz"

Kurt Brecht

"Gertsman has invented new spatial configurations; his galaxy spins out along a path forever balanced between imagination and reality, as between earth and sky."

Kristian Feigelson,* *Zoom* Magazine, August 1987

----

* Dr. Kristian Feigelson, Professor of Cinema, University of the Sorbonne, Paris, France.

SYMBOLS

Slowly I look at the monument, a symbol of Holocaust Museum Houston (page 66). The artist [Uri Kelman] who created the monument believes in good, the world, and the sun in the sky. The artist who photographed it caught the ray of the sun and the sky and the light on the gleaming surface of the monument and brought it to the people.

The theme of the Holocaust is subtly revealed in the exhibit of photographer/artist Valentin Gertsman in the Holocaust Museum Houston. Like everything in Gertsman's creations, the photographs combine color, composition, and extraordinary attention to detail.

"Detail, image" is probably the most accurate characteristic of his compositions: brilliant sunrays on the marble, the Philip Johnson skyscraper reflected in the raindrop on the hood of an automobile, or an eroded link of a prison bar fading into space.

The artist's uncanny gift for composition does not fit any known range of perceptions. His compositions are not born in his head. They are not based on knowledge of theory, if such knowledge exists at all. They come from his soul, from an exceptional feeling of space. Few people possess such a gift. All his creations are derived from that rare feeling for space. Precisely this is what removes his work from traditional photography and places it into the category of fine art.

One can confidently say that, thanks to Gertsman's creativity, photography begins to represent contemporary art form, where technical possibilities are unlimited and, possibly because of this, the synthesis of the composition – compositions not only of form but also of color – and performing technique becomes so important and attractive.

The artist leads the audience to the very meaning of the images he creates. This is a phenomenon, inherent only in true art, which removes artistic creations from the realm of craft.

Dr. Liya Pavlova

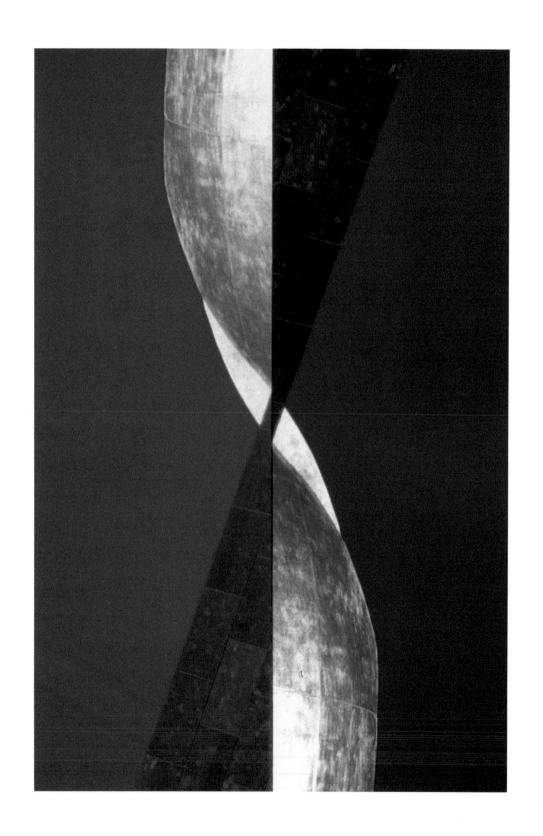

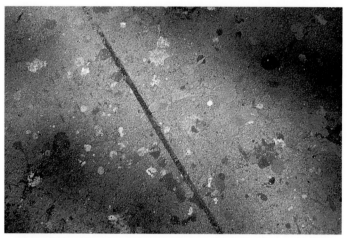

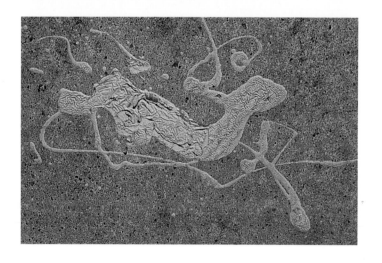

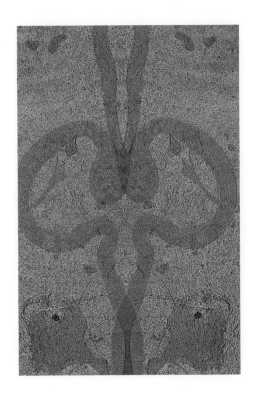  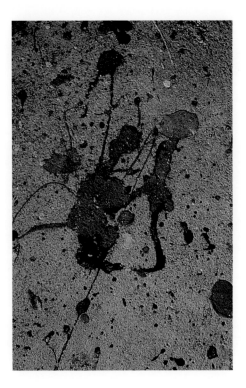

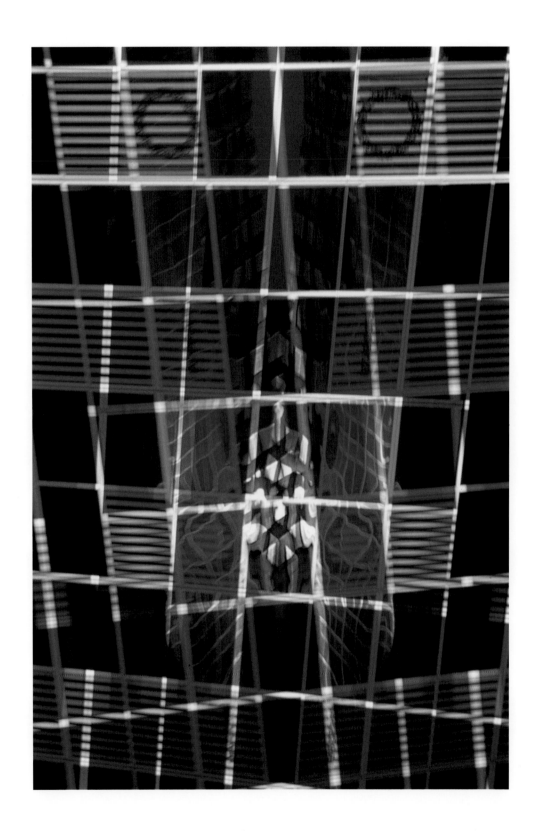

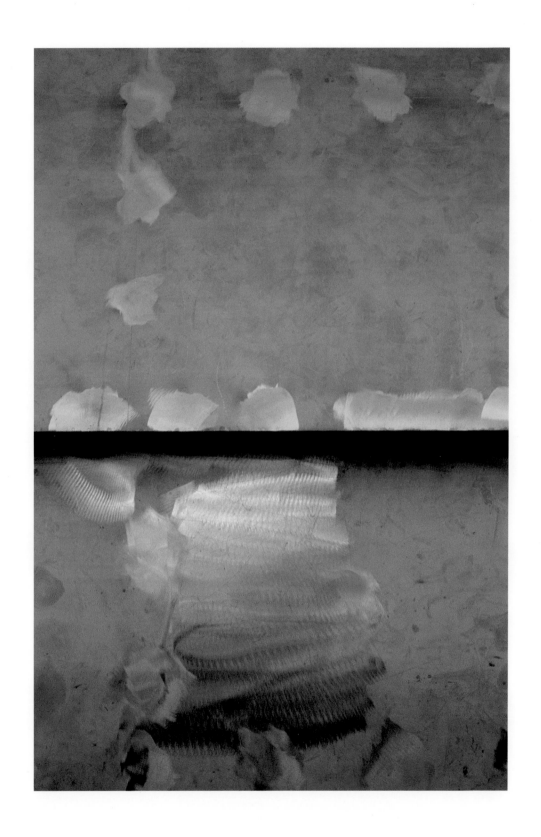

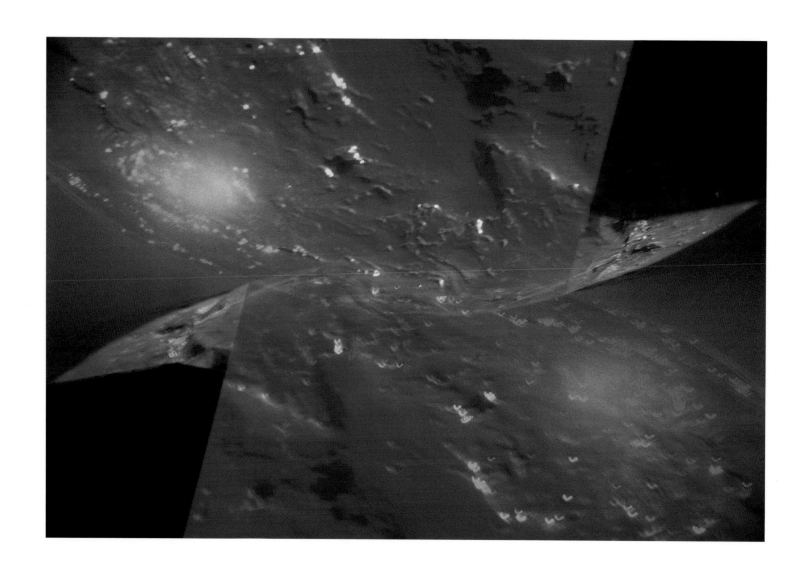

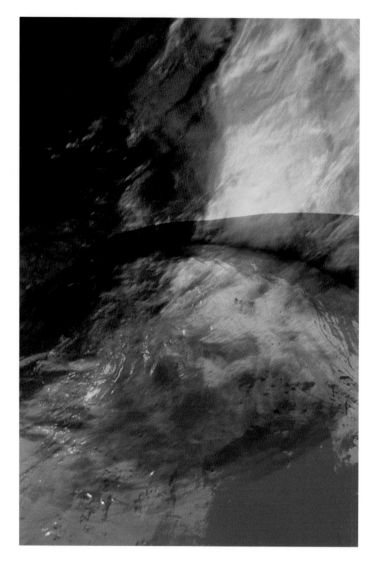

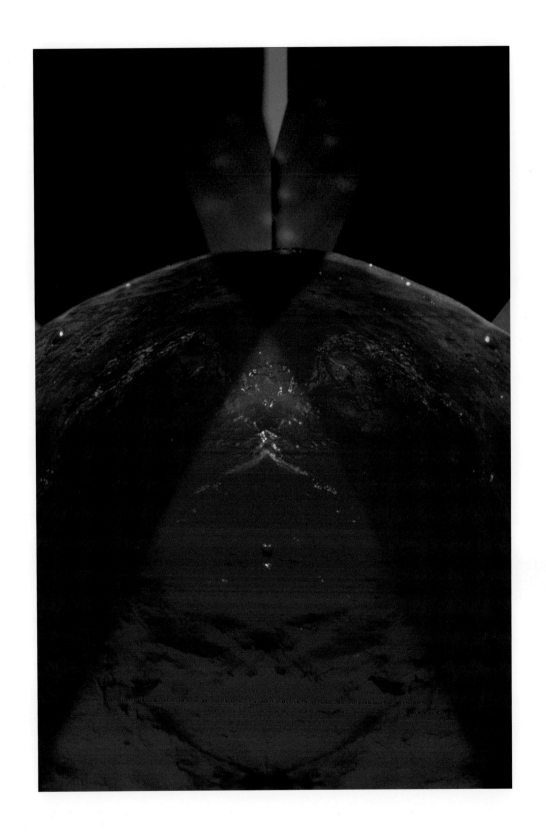

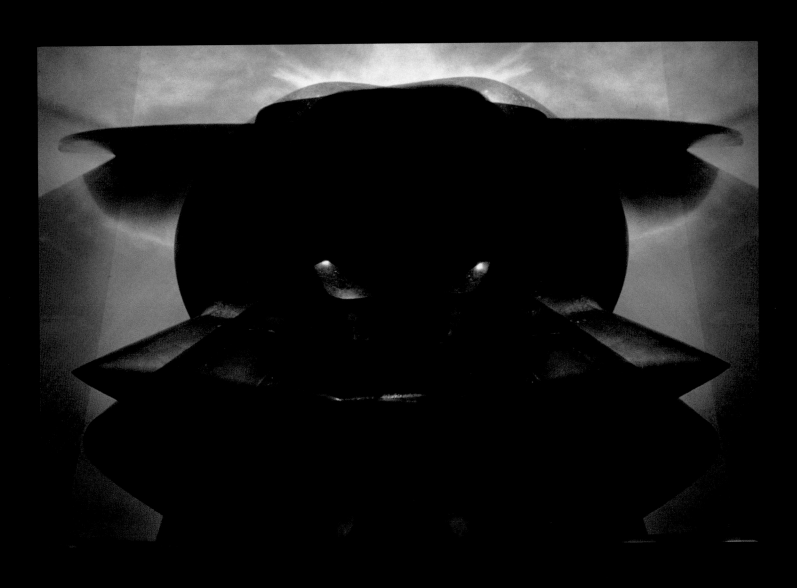

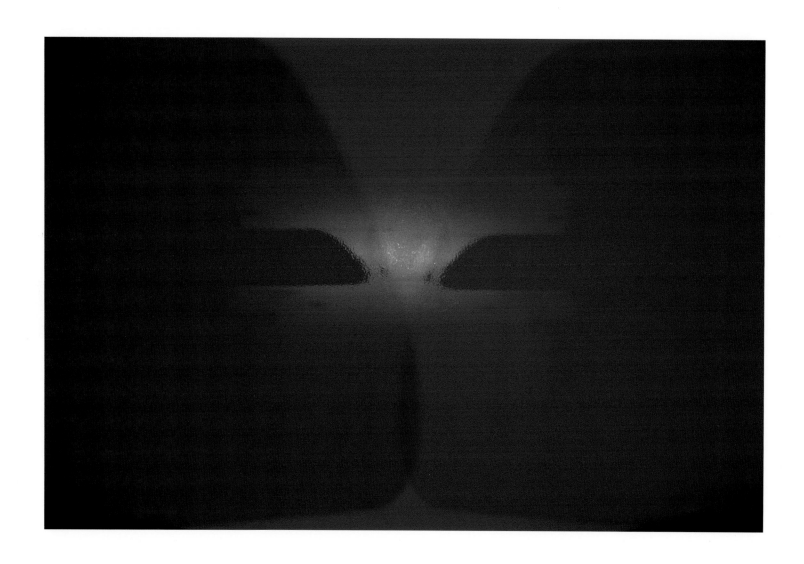

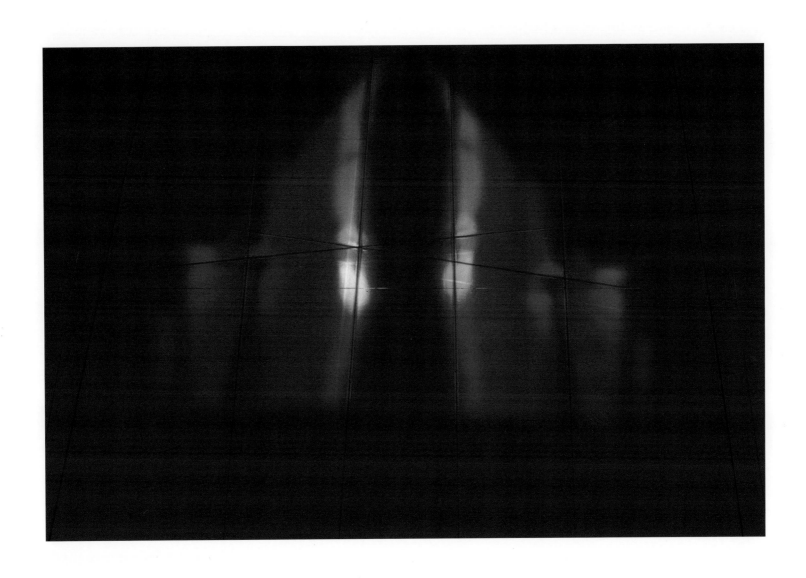

IN CONCLUSION

Gertsman's art is eminently spiritual, surging from a soul free from the technical concerns that would require the participation of reason. The critics may wish to busy themselves so as to supply the intellectual force needed to explain the optical miracle. Let the observer be a participant in a ceremony of pure feeling.

As a beautiful woman when contemplated, Gertsman's art does not call for interpretation but rather for unconditional emotional surrender.

Marcel Molina, M.D.

INDEX TO PHOTOGRAPHS

ACKNOWLEDGMENTS

I want to thank the people whose support and encouragement helped me develop my artistic career including:

Margarita B. Aksenenko, Doris Anderson, Virginia Anderson, Irina A. Antonova, Congressman Bill Archer, Edward A. Bader CSB, Leo Barenbaum, Bob Barrett, Nella Bielski-Cournot, Leon Bloom M.D., Yves Bosio, Catty Bosse, Pat and Bill Bradley, Betty Lou Brecht, J.V. Brook, Mayor Lee P. Brown, Willy Brui, Lucia Bryan, Kathryn Casey, Dr. Louis Chen, Jacques Clayssen, Martin Cominsky, Lucien Creusot, Kathryn Davidson, Susan Davidson, Dr. Rolf Denker, Jean Dethier, Cheryl Drasin, Dina and David Dukach, Gail Eissler, Madeleine and Claude Ernoult, Kristian Feigelson, Peter A. Fischer, Dr. Ines M. Flores, Efim Frumin, Viktor V. Gertsman, Julia van Haaften, Dewayne Hahn, Hon. Christin Hartung, Manuela Hoefer, Ann Holmes, Barry L. Horwitz M.D., Hon. Helen Huey, Fr. Janusz Jhnatowicz, Michael Jorden, Anatoly Kaplan, Alex Karcovsky, Barbara Karbarbi, Uri Kelman, Dennis Kiel, Pat Kiley, Jim C. Kollaer, Natalia Koltsova, V. Krutikov, Uri Kuper, Mayor Bob Lanier, David R. Legge, Jean-Claude Lemagny, Alex Levine, Konstantin Litvak, Kathryn E. Long, Joerg W. Ludwig, Ambassador Jack and Rebecca Matlock, Dr. Luis Matteo, Margarethe van Mayerhafer, Arlene McCarty, Susan Hallsten McGarry, Dr. Marina Menshikova, Gerd Meuer, J. Michael Miller CSB, Marguerite Milloud, Alexander N. Misharin, Dr. Reinhold Misselbeck, Martha C. Murphree Hon. AIA, Bart Nay II, Julia M. Nelson, Louis Neuray, Patricia Oliver, Eugin A. Olshansky, Mikko Pekari, Jacqueline Pontello, Glenda Regenbaum, Irvin J. Reiner M.D., Logan Rimes, Anna and Lev Rozin, Dr. Mikhail G. Rudin, J. Armin Rust, Ivor Safro M.D., Vera Safro, Carlos Sanchez, Manuel Santos, Adrian M. Shapiro, J. William Sharman Jr., Jeff Sirabella, Sally Sprout, Sonia Tabarovsky, Riyad Abu-Taha, Jerry Tasian, Oksana and Kirill Tatarinov, Bobby Taylor, Charles Thomas, Hon. Robb Todd, G.J. "Jordy" Tollett, Oleg Tselkov, Anne Tucker, Bob Tutt, Maria V. Valaeva, Kermit Veggeberg M.D., Yakov Vinkovetsky, Alkis Voliotis, John E. Walsh, Jr., Mayor Kathy Whitmire, Jerry Wilkenfeld M.D., Paul Winkler, Nabel Zabak, Mark and Elena Zaltsberg.

A very special thanks to John Berger, Kurt Brecht, Marcel Molina M.D., Gerald Moorhead FAIA, and Dr. Liya Pavlova, who put their talent and heart into their essays in this book.

Valentin Gertsman

CONTRIBUTORS

JOHN BERGER, born in London in 1926, is well known as an art critic, novelist, and screenwriter. His many works of fiction and nonfiction, innovative in form and far-reaching in their historical and political insights, include *Ways of Seeing, Art and Revolution, The Success and Failure of Picasso, To the Wedding, About Looking*, and *G.*, for which he won the Booker Prize. Among his books on photography is *Another Way of Talking*. Berger lives in a small rural community in the French Alps.

KURT BRECHT, a singer and songwriter, was born in Los Angeles in 1961. After beginning his studies in graphic design at the Art Institute in San Miguel de Allende, Mexico, he continued at the Art Institute of Houston. Since 1983 Brecht has been the lyric author and singer with his band, D.R.I. They have produced numerous tapes and CDs and toured North America, Europe, and the Far East. His life as a poet has led to the publication of several books of verse, *See the Loud Feeling, Notes from the Nest*, and *Word War I*. Brecht lives with his wife and son on a ranch near Houston.

MARCEL MOLINA, M.D., born in Paris of Argentine parents, grew up in Buenos Aires, Argentina. He received a BS in chemistry from Duke University in 1953. He received his MD degree from Temple University School of Medicine in Philadelphia, Pennsylvania, in 1957. In 1962 he completed his residency in general surgery at the C&O System of Hospitals in Virginia with a thoracic and cardiovascular fellowship at the University of Virginia Medical Center in Charlottesville. In 1965 he entered the private practice of surgery in Houston. In early 1980 Dr. Molina conceived and introduced the Gastric Segmentation, a surgical procedure for the correction of Morbid Obesity. He is one of the world's leading experts in this field. During the course of his surgical practice Dr. Molina became acquainted with Dr. Gertsman and was soon captivated by his unique and extraordinary artistic eye through the camera's lens. Dr. Molina became an early sponsor of Valentin Gertsman's artistic career.

GERALD MOORHEAD, FAIA, an architect living in Houston, Texas, is recognized for excellence in architecture, architectural writing, and photography. He has been active as juror, curator, lecturer, and journalistic editor and critic. His architectural work has received numerous design awards and has been published in national and international journals. Widely known for his documentary photography, Moorhead has had photos appear in many exhibitions and many reside in private and corporate collections. First and second editions of the *Houston Architectural Guide* were published with more than a thousand photographs by Moorhead. He is a Fellow of the American Institute of Architects and the Architect Laureate of Kazakstan.

Dr. LIYA PAVLOVA, born in Baku, Azerbaijan, is professor of architecture at Moscow State University of Civil Engineering, Moscow, Russia. She lectures on the history of architecture and basic architectural planning and has developed a course, "Mathematical Modes in Urban Studies." Her international activities include lectures in the Department of Architecture in Sofia, Bulgaria; Institute of Architecture and Construction, Weimar, Germany; and in the International School of Architecture in Helsinki, Finland. Dr. Pavlova has many publications in Russia and abroad, including the book, *City – Model and Reality*. Dr. Pavlova combines architectural and pedagogical activities with work as an artist. Her etchings and watercolors have been exhibited worldwide, including in Houston.

ABOUT THE AUTHOR

Dr. Valentin L. Gertsman was born in Moscow in 1925, emigrated to the U.S. in 1974, and settled in Houston, Texas. Parallel to his medical career (Ph.D. in orthopedics), he began to exhibit his sculptures and photographs in 1981 on a professional level. His first cibachrome prints, based on Houston architectural images, appeared in his shows, "Houston: from Traditional to Abstract" in the Museum of American Architecture at Houston Baptist University in 1985 and, the following year, "Houston - Paris" at the Plaza Gallery in conjunction with Houston FotoFest '86.

Since then, his exhibits of Houston images have been shown across the United States and Europe, including Le Palais de l'Europe, Menton, France; Espace Canon, Paris, France; Amerika Haus, Berlin, Germany; Salon Beaumarchais, Hotel de Paris, Monte-Carlo, Monaco; Central House of Architects, Moscow, Russia; Caseta Exposición, Del Recinto Colombino, Huelva, Spain, in conjunction with Fiestas Colombinas 1994 (502 years since the discovery of America by Columbus); Rotunda, Cannon House Office Building, Washington, DC; and in Houston at Rice University during the 1990 Economic Summit of Industrial Nations, Jones Gallery at the University of St. Thomas in conjunction with FotoFest '98, at Holocaust Museum Houston, and at the Museum of Printing History. Many of Gertsman's photographs are in public and private collections in such museums as Palais Carnoles Municipal Museum, Menton and Bibliotheque National, Paris, France; Museum Ludwig, Cologne, Germany; the Collection of The Vatican, Vatican City, Vatican; the George Bush Presidential Library & Museum, College Station, Texas; Tretyakov State Art Gallery and Pushkin State Museum of Fine Arts, Moscow, Russia; and The Menil Collection and the Museum of Fine Arts, Houston.

Photo by John E. Walsh, Jr.

Gertsman's photographs have appeared in many publications, including *Zoom*, international photographic magazine; *Southwest Art Magazine, U.S.A.*; *Traverses*, the publication of the Georges Pompidou National Center of Art and Culture, Paris, France; *Frank*, an international journal of contemporary writing and art; and *Society*, the magazine of the Sociéte des Bains de Mer, Monte-Carlo, Monaco. His Houston images also appeared on the covers of the last four issues of *Architecture USSR*. Since 1997 he has had close professional ties with the magazine *New Russia*, formerly *Sovetsky Souz* (Soviet Union), which has systematically published his work.

Dr. Gertsman has been recognized for his outstanding artistic contribution to the city by Houston's mayors Lee P. Brown, Bob Lanier, and Kathy Whitmire.